T0368702

# A Frothy Place in an Empty Space

## Momentoes

Ellen Ravelli

authorHOUSE

AuthorHouse™
1663 Liberty Drive
Bloomington, IN 47403
www.authorhouse.com
Phone: 833-262-8899

Published by AuthorHouse  02/14/2025

ISBN: 979-8-8230-4387-8 (sc)
ISBN: 979-8-8230-4386-1 (e)

Print information available on the last page.

This book is printed on acid-free paper.

Because of the dynamic nature of the Internet, any web addresses or links contained in this book may have changed since publication and may no longer be valid. The views expressed in this work are solely those of the author and do not necessarily reflect the views of the publisher, and the publisher hereby disclaims any responsibility for them.

# *Working The Time*

A little ash
On the plate
Is working like time

All the long gowns
Are crushed like bad silk
That we wore to a party.

Like the twelve reasons,
Like octagons and triangles,
The place was spared.

There was a time
When we were older,
There was no cure for cancer
And so many were
Not even born
Into these tall structures,
And there was no mirth
And blood filled strong men,
There was no one around.

# Water is Lost

Old water
    Sullies clothes,
        On the window
A petered out storm
        Settles down,

Into the fires
        Of hell
A giant sells his soul.

It is like lost furniture
           Found
In these frames
    Like pictures
        Of youth.

I would know better.
I cannot explain it,
Nobody told me.
I would find the salty potatoes,
        Cuckoo cuckoo
Goes the same old clock.

# World without End

Maybe it is a lot of cupcakes
This little life,
Born out of honor.

The silver toes shake,
How can it be this precious.

Like i wore armor
That day i bought chocolate,
No One could save it.

I claim there is nothing.

The weather
The weather
Goes into a split at the top of the world
And the end is a stay that flopped
And all that could be told.

# *Food*

Of late I sit
With no movies
And cry in my sleep.
I wish I would end smoking
And the bible is dry
Like the woodchuck
In my bathroom.
Service is for sinners
Where politicians meet
With thumbs up, hurting.
The bible is wet
Unlike the cue-balls
Taken out of context
In the night.
I drank some fudge
And pain was smeared with
Laughter because of a cold case
Of yellow broth
And a throat on fire.


O goofy goo
And the wrong way to health.

# Where is Bill

Who would live life alone
Holding cigars
And mailing out film
That could not be traced.

I put up a frame
At three in the morning
And fill out the cares
On the roads
To william
And going to the sea.

It is a pity
The signs signal a frost
And the movers
March on the rivers
By the gorge that has snapped
Like the soup in their throats.

# When It was Cold

Marked all over by skids
Of frozen jello,
I ate a tangerine in that
Hope and pretended it
Was it's stone model.

I am dressed to take it out By
entering an adventurous
Land, all the way to the Seine
In the back of a cruiser.

A singer of lines
In the war of reminiscence,
I kick a ball around a lake
And wake up to bloody ice on the blinds.

# He Knows

| Pockets | and | pops |
|---|---|---|
| | The Lord knows them, | |
| Grey | and | between |
| Fingers | | that entwine |
| My wrists | as | the stove caught fire. |
| I am soft | | on a rock. |
| The grand piano | | speaks |
| Livid | and | red |
| I hit | | my nose |
| | On willows | |
| In a field | | of flowers |
| | The Lord knows | |
| Relations | | are strained. |
| I wish | | my self |
| | Would end | |

# I Want Therefore

I want
  I want
    Therefore
     All grey is gone
It moves ahead
       To a splendid lawn
By a force of nature
  Needing a rest Once
    wearing a smile Is
      feeling sick
And the cows are closed
    They have no furniture
      It is past
And the lingo of the trade
     Needs a rest.

# *August is Like the Dawn*

August is like the dawn
     And there is a fresh face
     At my window.
   The sort of song
     That gets squished
     Before the final night
     Rises
And is dead like leaves.

     Persons promenade
To the scace buildings
     In the rain. Men
     open doors
To Radio City.
     I am like wood,
I cannot imagine
     The noise in my head.

There is lingering sorrow
     Like sugar cane,
Poor ones smile
And dissolve like water
     In coffee
     And rapid fire in war.

# *War on the Way*

The windows on the store
Are restored to rapid fire,
Like the shadows of slime
Of a monster,
A pack of dogs resemble soldiers.

Mister sold our hope
Like a gala of flamingos
In leather to the whereabouts
Of which we do not know.

The little glue
Which I knew of you
Is gone,
War is on the way,
To give us a side glance
Through the rain
By the bitter glow
Of these lines that
Are perishing between the sounds of joy.

# *What of Innocence*

Innocence is dead.
The strangled sugar
Is on the floor.
I take the prescription
To be a follower of Christ,

And see the bed markings,
Lord, let me sleep on air.

When sentences stopped
A mighty sky locked up
To make it's fat markings
Above my window.

More clothing was fried
In the rain.

And my sleep wear was mystified
Like being in a tunnel
Without a door, Living in a barrel.
I did not see anything
Although i tried.

# Games

Odors
   In the night
The logs are stubbed
    There is no fire
On the twelfth street
    A burning smell
Took the cue
    From the south.
The mail is lost
    In this train of thought
Pulling all the cords
      Out of the flames
To the wetlands.
    I will go for a breakfast.
    It is the same refrain.
    It is the same game.

# *Quakes*

Without a word
         The little room is on fire
On a clear night
    A sparrow drops
       And cries
There is silence
In the same rubble
       Between the gates
Of a mansion.
  The lawn will rip
Its insides in a grave
  When the quake stops
Its clothing,
There will be soot.

Wolves are called
Like dim fixtures
Like light bulbs,
They fall like trade winds
Near the sea in summer/

# The Factor

The white house glistens
          In the pink
It has fire escapes
And a way of accomplishment.
I saw it so and it was so.

On a grey day
Words turned into pretzels
For the tongues
On their own by the lake.

My purse got snatched
In the twilight
Of their songs
Being carried at midnight

Is this a con of life,
To be whacked
On the head by day,
Empowered by calico
Like lost hardships.

# Remembrance

I remember,
  Hogs would put on a face
  In an undergarment.
  It is like an overlook
  To passage to heaven,
  Money is squeezed......

Pull out that wallet,
The songs have ended
Like dry spice on a plate
Of spaghetti,
The wood fire
Explodes into bigger
Shares of green.

The allotments
Are folded like texts,
Like goats we go
Into sounds,
Like cranes
And the pull-out word factores.

# Down Home

Shine on,
     Chilli and pizza.
All would drop down.

Maybe, like rain on culture
A beagle sniffs my shoes.

I exclaim,
I am terrible in the same vein as wool.

No expulsion of teas
From the perpetrators of love.

My name is the same
On spots below
Face cream and the
     Forgotten summer.

All is dead
All is white
In this kitchen of hilarity.

# Britches

Monster-flesh
Is filtered out into the sea
By the bridge
By the town,
Like a tragic tree
Washed up into a fish
Lost beings find their house
One would guess
They will be devoured
By a galaxy.

Lost child.
We were told so
Who could weave a ray
Out of that maze by itself
Choking a liver.

Who would have took that work,
Born crumbling on its side.
Will the weather rain outside
And I dragging my feet
To seek a crown
Or some other perimeter.

# The Sun Also Sits

Chuck the Duck
Bends sideways
Down purple stairs
Absolutely empty.

Hang on to the guard rail
Entwined between roses,
Bitter north springs up,
This time love is gone.

We stood perplexed
And played a shell game
Before it was dawn,
Sweat rolled before our eyes,
It was broken
And limbs were shattered
Going down with the sun.

# Friends

Friends are spiffy,
They take off like cranes
Like a valuable teacher
So long songs,
The gifts of Christmas
Linger in the kitchen.

They absolve me
Of wear and tear
And the bite of filling leaves.

I opened then like a can of beer
And glory is struck.
Postmen are my friends
Like the grass of winter
Like a stillbirth in winter
Under the houses and trees
And the glee of Christmas.

# Express

There is nothing to express on impressions.
The wind-world dovetails magical messages,
I look into pancakes and there are riddles.
Mollified, packages of the mind are weird.
All those midnights, when soup was mixed
In a wagon to a great temple,
Gentle deeds done in sunny mush,
Eaten, as by a dog.

# *Pagan Smiles*

So smooth
And so like soot,
The black house
On the hill
Is ruined in spring
Beside the quick water.
A column of white
Is gallant for me
And it burns
Through a game
Of chance,
Like a wave of purgatory
And the small whispers
Of ten children
Out in darkness,
In the folds of firmness
And great spring.
They got up
And ate themselves
Of late like vegetables

# Everyday

This legal drip
Spiraling down
In the peculiar night
It is like ear wax,
The rest of it made up
Like a story about trials.

It is hard like potatoes.
My grave smile is brief
When I absorbed
Myself about living
At all costs.

So silent and so
Pretentious like make-up
On the face of a clown
When the force of coffee
Dripped like a ton
Of cola and other collections
Spread themselves for the asking.

# Patchworks

The night
   A patchwork
      Of mist
Is noise
  That cannot yell.
  We brood
To find calm
  When the seas
     Roll away
Into a thunder
   Like stillness.
Morning will slow
Its light
  And hide it's face,
  Again the lawns
Will shed and cry
To be made whole
    Like sanity
    Like the penmanship
  Of a child

# *Fridays*

Just that it would end
The banging at the door
And the blue haze.
It ends up in the dirt,
A cracked tooth in a barrel,
So it would kill poetry,
There is no thought to it.

Some grew their grains
In deposits on the ground,
Above winter was fixed
To dry the words.
It begins and ends
In the desert.

Just what I figured,
The power ran dry
And flames perished
By the gates
To bones and worms
And outerwear.

# Mommy

The sound of dusk
Carries me over
Into the strains of air,

Like a forest on fire
Twelve stars gravitate
Toward the rain.

Minutes fall like a ball
In confession, a bird sings.
Lighthouse goes down
Like a rock.

I marvel at the weather.
There is no spartan trust
Between my reflexes
To the water on the roads.

My memory would
Be ignoble if it
Were it not for
The tot's tattle of woe
Outside my door.

# New England

The pine of New England
Is like no other.
See the trees
Through caves in woods,
A little shell with it's drops,
Picks up its peaks
And moves towards channels
In the sea.

A word to the atmosphere
Is like ice
And a store of air.
The beating of hearts
Is here on the shore.
Is like black rain
With sounds in every corner.

# Seven Hills

A toy like a gift
Is broken
　The sad part
　　　Is spoken
　　　　　In kingdoms
And a little wood
　　　Is crimson
Like fellow travelers
　　　Who break the fall
　　　Like a waterfall.
I poised for more time
　　　In a village
　　　To run like a donkey
　　　　　In the sand
　　　　　Between carnage
　　　　　And the moon
And whatever quarry breaks up,
　　　　　Gone are kings
　　　　　Up seven hills

# Endings

We have won
And chosen sides
For love of angst.

The fortunate slave
Gives in to error
Their complex tirades.

It never ends,
Like a soldier's smile,
We look like peas

Of blue and red
And the gates
To the waves are closed.

For a miner 's touch
For the sweat of angels

The lapse of time
Burn and then discend
Like trash in a bin
On a sunny day.

# Great

The memories link to
The birth of Christ
Are satisfied and waiting.

There are no grim spoils,
Like a bad tooth
We set down to dinner
Of pork and franks.

And found candy,
It filled us like spices,
I kicked back
And had gone to sleep.

Waiting for the departure
Of that train
At midnight
At the close of bars
And games.

How sad for old friends,
Thinking of Dickens
And the paramount.

# Ahead

O go ahead
    Ahead of me
    Into the nest
    Where there are vipers
    And snakes.

You wear a bland smile
And give into precedent
And moral expense.

My heart is pressed down
    In my chest,
There are no words for it.

We were like strangers in a hotel
    And noone cared,
    For the life of me
I will never know it.

I will hum like a ham
And fall down a drain
When I hear that song
Not far from the shore
And the weird tides,
O I've lost a million beans.

# Mountain Adrift

Onry notion-
What will do with my days,

A paramount surprise
Love lingers on red squares,

Like polish on a glass of milk. Mortal
seasons run over

The airy testing places
Of the deep like the seas

Moving it's wits,
I alone see the strengths

Of having a bunch of apples
To cook or aim

At the mountain of drifts
In my lungs.

# Do Tell

Breaks in the river
Run like the river
Dunking the structure
Like gallons of ice
For tea on a hot summer's day.

Momentary leaves are greener
In a handy fish-net of trees
That waste like stores.

Until crocus spring like
Pagentris of truth
Lawyers give quarters of green
In the serenity,
Marked splinters of rock
Shiver like hustlers.

# The Bay

The port of Montigo
Is better than an isle
In faraway scenery.

The little children
Blame the noise
In the foghorn wail
Like a bad regiment.

They swing over their peril,
Who watches the red light of blue,
Moments are marvels in the sea.
We carry on the day

With instant homage to green alligators.
Winds to the west generate fire-eyes
And a pained touch of grey.

# Milo

Green Milo wanders around
Spitting up cough drops
Born on the occasion of Christmas
In a newly populated desert.

Springs of triumph
Like lions in the leaves
Are snarled like hair,
Blood is written on his rewards.

One finger in the wind,
Is drowning under stars,
Everyone loves the magic mirror.

Hail the winners,
Hail the laughing ducks,
I see the finest donnybrooks
On the streets.

# Dust to Dust in Memory

How long before the years grow deep
In the premature hours.
Solitary illusions sprinkle
Like rain over dust.
Worlds are in the making,
Angst in reflections in playgrounds,
Those tendencies to grab everything
Like fodder from hungry cows are gone.
The smells of fresh clothing let go
Like triggers triggering small talk
Around the table.

Monuments are made of beer and song
Walked by near churches that
Ring bells like bowling balls
In the intermission of rain.

# Northern Lights

The northern lights and their green
Bemuse children with special attitudes
Knowing the altitude of creatures in mists.

Solid rock in clocks is swelling in the murky
Solstice of winter.

Did my sister go to Boca Raton to
Play cribbage and eat pineapple
In palm trees and sand.

I will ask the all-knowing moat
To castles in the air.

# The Wild West

I get up on the caffeen,
Rising like a tailor.
I am sunk like the mattress.
I am part of the problem
As I pull out a gun
And walk into the dark. The
goods shock the sky, Hung
like a sea of redress.

Down below are
Spinoffs of Elvis,
Pounds for a grain of sand,
Spawned by murders of pronouns
And manly Santa Clause
Ahead like Christmas,
The beginning of rising bread.

# Paris-City

Feeling boxed in and sizzling,
There are the statues of gals
Maypoles in the face of creation.
The little Paris-city tastes like
A cookie in its undies.

I am boxed in,
Caressing the stripes of a log.
I will burn my future
And clear my scalp of winners
Peeling an apple while the foghorn
Goes pop in a cell of conclusion.
I am outwardly out like a king-pin.
Having collected stone mounds of wind.

# Writing Poetry

Ping is naked and alone,
Zing, I am here on a ledge,
Below are the tacks.
I will complete my chores
Made in the seas,
In the poems of May.

The tame waves are gone
And so are the penny citations
On my windows.
It is a good spring,
Declares the champagne.

Women wear clothes on all pounds of flesh,
Mother eats lobster with churned butter
From the coast of Maine,
Writing on my ears like a telegram.

# The Beach

The pain of those people,
They were weathermen
Suddenly on glossy peaks.

Energy senses move downward.
Every fiber in the maze is obscure.
I play the pounding with little pleasure.

Golden sun is situated in high minutes.
My wrecked reflexes given to a child.
Withering rays of drama
Plague the place like wrestlers,
My back lies on a plain
Toward the shore to be like seamen,
Insulated like treasure.

# State of Mine

One morning fog flew past my sight,
Heck,
The fog flew past in a dream.
he dream was a caravan,
Semi-dry.
Gpd left furnishings in a state,
My state by the sea.

I was master of my shadows,
Eating the sprout.
Icing on the wall.

I opened a jar to the sea
Finding a meaningful donor
In a shut dream,
The loose descent to decency
In the fountain of His glory.

# Yellow Patches

The late diver crams his neck
Into a spiral of bleeding down.
Sodden wood in the caves
Of yellow patches in town are grim,

Pleides mills about the woods
In special spring,
The given conclusion
Is more than a trapezoid.

It is a pain in the neck
That faces me and the squirt,
When Maine is a jumpstart
Away by the lake where my boat is.

# Many

The eyesore of the building
Has been vanquished
Between veils of myopia.
In a fridge arena is blazing winter.
On a school bus children
Ruminate like clients.
Fat cows are spawned from the clouds
Killers of little people in their homes
Who dress merrilly
With eyes shut before spring comes
With its dangerous hollows.
Nobody can wait in shirtsleeves
With a high fever
For a frozen popsicle.

# Collision

Such a chemical collision,
Two cars popped the lanes
In a sultry maze.

One pointed east in the decision
To ramble by evening.
The good guitar sang

In all the pressure of being bent
Like the wonder of exclusion
Traveling the east.

As if gossamer-wings
Of doves sparked the wind.
It is a fair assumption.

Joe stole the polaroid film
From the tree sitting as a bystander
To a frightful fixed night
With haunted joints.

# Business

Nothing will bring back the spring.
Owners are nonplussed
In a phase of rapture.
Mornings kitchen soothes
Heartaches that will not stop.
By gosh, I have more tendency
To lye down like a toad
Skipping over higher positions.

I heard in time locations
In the atmosphere are like dangling string.
The bottom capsized like a vessel,
Gone overboard like it's pattern
That is the same in another light.
I pay top dollar for a summery
Which we like to read of long ago
In a long term operation.

# Estates

In high estates a pale tongue
Is icy like spots on the rug.
The right shimmering star
On the horizon acts like
A glaze of yellow

The spoof on the roof
Is like guns of terror,
Spots of green roses
Melt in the shade
Excusing the scent.

Children look like snowy down,
As they finger for the locks
On ice, spoiled twice
In the race to ecstacy.

# *Treasure*

Windows of treasure
Like windows of opportunity
Gravitate like the wind.

Miles of leisure assuage like gold
Personhood will go up in a cup.

To bring to the house
These moods of the king,
Debunked like water,

Carried to the gates
With special graves,
Unknown to noone were the origins,

Spastic pulling east and west
Like the great wheat in the yard.

# Tree

High tree like a high chair
Rocks like music.

The salad on my spoon is sweet.
Tomatoes do not pay
Claims of the grass
Once strained in late autumn
Between the feet of dogs.

Leaves fall like tulips
On the silver screen of sky. Pits
of frost pummel the glen
Aberrations on the way to earth.

# Salt of Noise

The sound and rush in fragments
Is spoiled like knives.
The great white smell
In a posh seat is like
A spell of poison.

Grandstanding crowds yell
Out much in the dark.
Boss broke the furniture
Like songs of the open heart.

The suits of those men
Are yellow in the back,
Explaining themselves,
As they look for packages
In the rain
In the cold of asphalt
In the salt of rain.

# Questions

Orange coral and white
Connections are over church towers
The snow is hitched to potholes.
I sit out and reach for a flame.
A partaker of cheese.
I sift through the mail
And bend like drum.

They would say I am finished
And starting to reverse In
the pale light of noon
That peers over us.
Trees are solid like oars
In the burning questions
Of the ages.

# Red

Redundancy flies into a red house,
Below the map of weapons,
And a lenient pipe pops.

I was married to a good king
And the fallen mop
That was preyed upon.

I wiped furniture.
It was below zero
On the first year calendar

There is no stake in misfortune,
Says the carry-out fliers.

A bottle of soap
Was slippery and on target
For the beginners of begging
For all in an ice storm.

# That Sound

The gas fumes from Nova Scotia
Are redundant on the pass
Between rural homes.
On constant slopes the watersheds
Drain in the aftermath of
Constant fever and strife,
Roads less taken lead to
A universe of passion
By the fair flags on the steps
Of my porch.
I look for warmer weather
In the spring, alone, and
Without cares carrying the
Frozen rum in baskets
With towels for the future.

# Points Lost

The silent sliver
In the side
Is like fog-dust
In the cans of neighbors.

I brought down a spotted owl
With balls.

The clientals of fashion
In the wind hinders
The light use of shapely skies.
Above the windows,
On the roof,
Are solitaire players.

The positive points
To their con
Are between my fingers As
love was lost in winter Like
statues giving up coins.

# *Triumph*

The patches on their eyes
Are hazardous to the
One momentary schooner.
I go where there is no leer.

A sparkle of triumph
In the ripped wind
Is like songs of autumn
Between hours of sunset.

The tame measure of God
Are explosive
Like the soldier's delight,
Of three mornings
Above the trappings of fire.

# In the Morning

Nut buns and cakes sitting on the sills
Are battleships with a penchant
For glory in the sand.
I could have died in the tavern.
It is a mood of depression,
The cat calls and mastermind
In the streets are like streams of water.
The sudden stimulation of tires
Is like bypass surgery.
There is bread to bake in the evening
By that time I will have awoken.

# Little Sheets

The noonday forces quicken
To the likelihood of
Para-adventure
In the salty maze of a beach.
My wind swept hands are cold
Like mildew when I reach for baby.
The little sheets of gold
Fold a fire almost bubbling like wood.
I ask of life the light
Pointlessly fixed on the wall
And pet the palpable
Goats of a stranger.

# Government

The psycho tick is the same on every rug.
By law it is established.
Like the houses without frames.

Truly goodness in life Is in
the barnyards Through
the countryside.
Parenthesis are the same in the rain.

The government says it is legal to wipe out
The trees and pull down the shacks,
With the steeples before evening comes
And mirth is run over.

# *Sparkles*

The go to of a swamp
Is a mill in the sun.

My gray hair and a
Knife in the kitchen
Are like southern winds.
This spiral convoy
Goes to a conclusion.

The paramour of my heart
Is rife like a tabloid.
Solitude is like a gun
In a premier at home.

On the winter sky
The lark of fortune
Curbs my appetite
For the angry young men.

In the sands of Los Vegas,
The sky breaks.

# Everyday

This legal drip
going down
In the peculiar night,
It is like ear wax,
The rest of it made up
Like a story about trials.

It is hard like potatoes.
My grave smile is brief
When i absorbed
Myself about living
At all costs.

So silent and so
Pretentious like make-up
On the face of a clown
When the force of coffee
Dripped like a ton
Of cola and other collections
Spread themselves for the asking.

# Remembrance

I remember,
Hogs would put on a face
In an under-garment.
It is like an overlook
To passage to heaven.
Money is squeezed.....

Pull out that wallet,
The songs have ended
Like dry spice on a plate
Of sausage
The wood fire
Explodes into bigger
Shares of green.

The allotments
Are folded like texts,
Like goats we go
Into sounds,
Like cranes
And the pull-out word factors.

# Pagan Smiles

So smooth
And so like soot,
The black house
On the hill
Is ruined in spring
Beside the quick water.
A column of white
Is gallant for me
And it burns
Through a game
Of chance,
Like a wave of purgatory
And the small whispers
Of ten children
Out in darkness,
In the folds of firmness
And the great spring.
They got up
And ate themselves
Of late like vegetables.

# *Friends*

Created and centered
    But not like a
vegetable, I put a carrot
in my ears,
    It crinkled
    And snapped
In my heart,
There was one
suckered. Could
there be more
    Creatures at this
point, The line of
thunder
    Is like a ball of
thunder In the poor
people's houses. Is it
more cozy
    To be certified
    And scared of the
       townspeople
    And the coming age
     And my pint made of glass
      And the silver on the table.

Printed in the United States
by Baker & Taylor Publisher Services